A New Kind of Country

A NEW KIND OF COUNTRY

KYLE SCHLESINGER

CHAX
TUCSON
2020

Grateful acknowledgment to the editors of the following periodicals for publishing some of these poems: *Aural Literature; Banqueted; Beautiful Mutants; The Brooklyn Rail; A Dozen Nothing; EcoTheo Review; Flash Code; Level Land; Newport Life; The Nightjar Review; Peach Fuzz; Southwestern American Literature;* and *Truck*. 'Up Close' appeared as a pamphlet from Breather Editions with art by Jolie Holland. 'True Story' is a picture-poem collaboration with artist Philip Trussell, and 'It's a Freak Out' is a picture-poem collaboration with Brad King. 'Beyond Repair,' 'Dream,' and 'Jumpshot,' were produced as limited-edition prints for Marfa Book Company. 'How Color Works' appeared in Nate Ethier's monograph *Wilderness*. Special thanks to c_L Books for publishing some of these poems as a chapbook entitled *Let's Drift*, and to the estate of Ted Greenwald for permission to publish our collaboration, 'None of Us.'

ISBN: 978-1-946104-25-0

Library of Congress Control Number: 2020942986

for Bernardine Dohrn, Bill Hicks,
Waylon Jennings, & Roberta Pedon

Without perishing from the tricks of my own mind, how would I get to Kingsley?
— Ride in the Whirlwind

It matters not where or how far you travel, the farther commonly the worse, but how much alive you are.
— Henry David Thoreau

And somebody said it was nice while it lasted.
— Emmett Grogan

CONTENTS

SOMETHING BEAUTIFUL

for John Godfrey

Think of something
Now think of something else
The green that is apples

Is the green you may recall
As you were saying
Where you kept putting it
Ring in wood reminds

A certain ring to it
Just then the buck stops
And everyone gets off

Behind twined years
Hum after the houselights
Come on and on again
Don't even go there

Outcast moon doesn't sound right
There's a table for two
Through the floating doors

Where air breathes in a small pond
Through cattails and sand
Where train tracks run forever
And trains we've never seen

Ambien summer storm
We brought our nets anyway
I retrace my steps in the dark

Write another sixteen-liner
And the air feels like my body
Like smoke and seaweed and
The streets are empty

Inside your body and it's
Wonderful being inside out
There's something else in the air

No one can touch or stay home
You clean the bathroom on
Sundays with the radio on
A transistor plain as day

It's times like these
When no one's around when
Trees are the weeds of winter

And there's a glow of
Green light in the snow

ALL SEASONS

It was all seasons at once, someplace like Vermont, and there's me, David, Brad, Hunter, Jamaica, and a few other friends from town. Areas of the ground are covered in snow partitioned into neat geometric areas, but the air is warm, the sun is strong, like the first day of spring and everyone's in a really great mood. There are patches of bright green moss and wildflowers, creating a kaleidoscopic pattern I can see from high, high above us. We're sitting on a small stage made of wicker and pallets, and the stage is on a drawbridge. I'm next to a big pile of pumpkins and Brad's at the other end of the stage meditating near a bale of hay. His eyes are closed and his posture is excellent. The rest of the group is laying on beach towels between us soaking up the rays. Everyone looks great wearing cut-off jeans, and the men are wearing leather sandals with their shirts off, while the women are wearing vibrant swimsuit tops and flamboyant plastic sunglasses. None of the men are wearing sunglasses, except for this one guy with a beard that I don't recognize. Brad sends me a telepathic message: I don't trust that guy in the sunglasses—keep an eye on him. Roger that.

David and Hunter are lost in conversation, David lying on his stomach, while Hunter stares up at the clouds. Since we're all in telepathic dialogue, we're sending each other images and responding to them with words aloud. Moments of silences come and go, and although to an outsider, it might appear that we're speaking in non-sequiturs, we've actually arrived at a dialogue of pure poetry. Off in the distance, we hear the sound of a tugboat's horn, a low, earthy drone, and then the call of the seagulls, and there's muted music in the air. I invite everyone to a poetry reading happening at 4:30. I'm digging everything and everyone, but there's a part of me that wants to leave, to drive through the Green Mountains alone, to feel the cool rush of the air and the wafting smell of spring mud coming down from the hills, driving into the sun. Hunter scratches his nose.

The sound of the tugboat is near, and suddenly, the drawbridge begins to tremble and there's a quickening of the heart. I snap out of my groove for a moment, and wonder why there isn't a whistle or a light alerting us that the drawbridge is about to open? David senses my concern on the instant, and tells me that if we all stay connected and centered, everything will be fine. We feel the shift in our equilibrium as the bridge begins to lift and our collective elation is growing. Everyone's smiling warmly at one another, except for that guy in the sunglasses and beard. The bridge is almost vertical now, and I make meaningful eye contact with a clockmaker across the street who has come out to watch the tugboat pass. He's seen it a thousand times. The bridge keeps lifting, rotating, shifting cranks and pulleys and I love these pumpkins so much that I connect with them as well to keep them from falling through space. Now we've ascended beyond the vertical, and we're coming down completely upside down, staring into the water, watching huge chunks of ice drift downstream.

START OVER

I spent a year on a farm
Trying not to freak out
And holding food down

Breathing and
Remembering to breathe
Waiting for the phone to ring

The door to knock
Or bust down
But mostly smoking

Listening to records
Fixing on small
Corners and edges

Forgetting names for
Colors and light and
Contrast that's distinct

From sullen irony and glances
And this week's been a rainy one
And there's a lot of great people

In town and lots of lightning bugs
Living with Chris old
Habits new routines and

WORDS

for Robert Creeley

The words are in the body
The body is in the mind
The big white cloud
Is in the sky

The stars are in the eye
There is a butterfly
On my finger

The heart is in the Bronx
There's 'nothing' 'in' Delaware
The brain is not the mind
The future looks bright

The chance is in
The forefoot
The money's under

The table
The suitcase is on
The mattress
Because nothing

Really mattress
The mistress
Has a mistress

The numbers
Don't add up
The money talks
The belly breathes

The words are in
The mouth
The tongue

Tickles the pizza
But the heart
Stays alive
The finger

Is in the ear
And the other finger
Is in the other ear

Because the dragon
Is in the moat
And 'emotion'
Is the caption

Beneath the moat
Beneath the caption
Below the words

Under the stars
That breathe in
A movie starring
An actress

From the
Twentieth century
Whose name escapes me

UP CLOSE

And the poets that has the best of everything
And the most that is a nothing better than a teaser
A scroll made of paper, a gold shiny piece of paper
They shall walk by fries in summer by a jar of many ones
I got a picture of gum that's special
Because it's a piece of treasure

PROVIDENCE

What's on television
Just another hallucination

We've got the volume at forty-five
To make the weather sound better

There's a place where Zepplin's always on
But we don't take the lyrics too seriously

Like Conrad's mom
And there's always a haircut

You don't understand
Donald Sutherland's voice

Ted Berrigan's Providence
The slant of the sleet

The grit of the street
Where there's a Duncan Donuts

On every corner
And then something changed

And everyone turned on the radio
Turned off the lights

And I wonder where you are
Where Huey's at

OKLAHOMA YAHOOS

I think I'm going crazy
In this jacuzzi
On the mesa

Pink lightning
Burnt sienna
The year is 1977

And outlaw country
Is way past its prime
High as a kite

The cue takes you
Balls burst into flames
Because there's magic

Then there's *magic*
Gasoline rainbows
Neon shimmer

Acid rain on
Ordinary asphalt
Reminds me of you

When you're very far away
I push the sky
That holds me in

ZOOM

Angels are ceilings
Sentience runs through
The floor

Dissolves

The part of the Polaroid
That's not the picture

The ghost in me sputters
The face is your face
Cool to the touch

CAPE COD, '89

Once removed we're watching
Hannah and Her Sisters
On the tube

Sunday afternoon motel room
And there's that chlorine
Hairdryer smell of seaweed
New carpet and nicotine

Midwinter days
But not in that order

There's a knock at the door
And a beautiful stranger
Climbs into bed with us

Without saying a word
The air is very blue
I guess everyone is crazy
About Hannah and Her Sisters

Hours pass and outside it's
Drizzling so a couple from

Tennessee gives us a ride
To a new bar in an industrial park
We're planning a wedding

Or that was the impression
Their van is *really clean*

Where there's music
I just want to kiss your face

To see if you want any more face
I've got the seedy taste of

Christmas in my mouth
Rain falls on our parade
Faded and clean

JUMPSHOT

for Tom Raworth

Before the flat a fifth
Ball to the wind
Pissing in paradise
Small stone eyes cast
Each day different gray
Hightops of youth
All you do is
Point and shoot

OFF THE HOOK

You wouldn't believe it
If I told you
That I was where
You thought you were
When we heard the news
Come over the wire
Seems like yesterday
Only yesterday
Seems like an eternity
And tomorrow's
Just around the corner
And every movement

There's a feeling
Of routine and possibility
That keeps me on my toes
Okay, since you asked
A little about me
Let's see, guilty pleasures?
For starters:
I love a new toothbrush
(especially orange)
And black t-shirts
Medium, 3-packs with
A pocket on the breast

But I'm not picky
I mean I am
But not really
After you get to know me

But enough about me
How about you?
Yeah, me too…
Oh totally…
Wouldn't be caught dead, etc.
Yeah, I see what you…
Those fucking pricks…
Say, now *there's* an idea!

Phone's ringing off the hook
Outside it's dark
And it's already been noon
For an hour, maybe two
Where does the time go?
And it's still dark outside
It looks like rain, and boy,
We could sure use it!
And I know you're coming
Over on your bike
In an hour or two
What will we do?

I'm a sincere person
(really mean that)
But I can't take life
Too seriously
And that sums it up
Pretty good
I think, I think
I take the phone
Off the hook
Look up at the sky
Close my eyes—
Now it's all coming back to me

SPLIT

We were
Now we're

NOT GOING

Not going
Just leaving

Wonder if they
Wonder about me

The way I wonder
About them

He still has that
Look about him

I REMEMBER SOMETHING YOU ONCE TOLD ME

Was it something I said?
Maybe something like
When I think about you
I quote myself.

My father always said
Put it in writing
But he isn't much of a writer
You were saying something

About the Rolling Stones
And I was holding the bag
Not insincere but just
Totally bungled because

History is mosaic and hilarious
I was a little stoned
Maybe making a sunflower
Someone once said

There's always a beautiful
Someone at Juice Land
And that's pretty much true
We were just getting started

So many things are extravagant
Even a perfect spiral
Because once is an idea
You can pounce upon

Jump up and down on the iota
I almost forgot to tell you
Hold that thought about
Perspective and all the cameras

Like cinéma vérité par excellence
There's someone on the other line
They're coming down here in a cab
Someone actually said that

IT'S A FREAK OUT

with Brad King

It's a freak out
In the peace temple

The line for brunch
Was a mile long

I erected bigger and
Taller until

A seagull perched
On a dumpster and

It became
The peace trap

SPENT

Spent the first half of the day
Clearing up the second half
Of yesterday

Spent the second half of the day
Cleaning up for tomorrow
In the future

Like they say

LAVENDER COUNTRY

We're somewhere on the Lower East Side, and it's early autumn, but *it's not the heat, it's the humidity,* Pacino whispers to me. A group of elderly people (Lewis, Anne, Bill, Lyn, Joanne, and Alice) are following me, because I, ostensibly, know where the church is at. No one resembles themself. I'm lost. Everyone's tired, overheated, running wicked late, getting irate. I'm feeling it, and suggest that we take a breather in the park, sit down in the shade. Tompkins Square is bonkers, nowhere to think straight, then I spot a spot on a bench next to guy in a nice suit: *can I sit here?* And he says, *fuck off,* not looking up from his phone. I lose it, grab him by the collar, throw him to the ground, kick in the ribs, stomp out the jaw. He is gone now, taking his body with him, when all the time, I thought it was the beauty of his mind I loved.

IF ANYTHING

Night is a duration
Then I forget
The opening act
Lunar past

Country talks back or
Something to that effect
If anything goes
Same here

Like a small ship
Like a small spillway
Little parts of the road
You can't take with you

First things first
Take a breather
Pack the Telecaster
Don't forget to write

ASLEEP IN THE ATTIC

Red, yellow, and green triangles
In the afternoon light school's a
Disappointment flunking optical
Geometry flickering egg on summer

Driving to the new age in a bathtub
Full of junk after dark with a redneck
Hippie, an elegant photographer,
Stokely Carmichael, George Wallace, SDS

The notorious Country Joe interview
What do you do with the real magic
All of sixteen, false raga shirt and jeans
Tabula rasa in the shade won't stay

Because a point in space is a place
For an argument insisting on emptiness
When there's no mind left to treat
Light moves slower through water than

Air refracting what stays or appears to
Toss a pebble in the water of meaning
And watch concentric circles form
Smooth as eyelids sure as uncertainty

As natural as miscegenation a feeling
That happens to get there then you
Arrive in a wild space material bliss
The ground shifts all the time as

Paradise must in every transformation
There's a want for clarity in the roar of
Sense making like a shape you just made
Up one afternoon asleep in the attic

PRACTICE SPACE

Make a practice space
Big enough for learning

Mind is a line
A point in space

Cast a ledge
Coast off

Bottom line
Full of free refills

Before uncertainty
There was practice

Don't make any
Sudden moves

LET'S DRIFT

Someone's out there
Dead horse horizon
Bluest of blues

And the brambles
Work the street
There's dusk then light

Dust and light again
And the dust got lighter
And lighter than dusk

Turned into dusk again
Someone's out there
Nothing's more beautiful

Than catching a wild hair
Does vinegar last forever
As far as the money goes

I don't have any
LSD and meteor showers
My friend was Sarah Hopper

She wore a green jumper
Like rough numbers
In the dark

Shoulder to the wheel
In baking heat
Bedrock of river

Coldest smoke in the pines
In the sun on horseback in
I remember everything

And when we get there
No Indian on the moon
No names on the moon

The moon people went away
Pills of the high planes
Round back they never

Two too many
Summer bands
Someone done

Gone and dosed
The well

ANY DAY NOW

The beauty of anarchy
Is that no one can agree
What to be but only
What not to be

The proximity of democracy
Once upon a cloud
From solid to liquid
And back again

Intensity doesn't equal audacity
I'll see your plasticity
And raise your enthusiasm
Any day now

PLANKS

There's sunbeams on the floorboards
It's never easy to say goodbye
With a Victorian accent
So I press my camera against the glass
And take a picture of an airplane
Inside there's someone I love
But the picture just looks like
Any old airplane
Like an emotional genius
And why do rivers have edges anyway
I can do that too just watch
A side project is a tall order

BEYOND REPAIR

Tree of life
Paradise lost
Tan line

DREAM

You know that
Feeling you get
The night before
A pet dies

That's exactly the
Way I feel before
The word appears
In the white rectangle

HELLO

It's so good to see you
You look so great
I didn't recognize you
How are things
Let's talk about notebooks
And the girls behind
The fence playing
Hide and seek

Let's talk about clouds
Without alluding to
Anything but clouds
Let's sing about poetry
Without mentioning
Any proper names
Let's describe the Crusades
Using colors only

Let's look out
At the tall grass
And look the other way
Go for a long walk
Notice all the things
We've passed
Through the years
Coffee cups, remote controls

Pens and maps
The only way to say a word
Without changing its meaning

May be *this in passing*
There's cedar in the air
And more besides
'What else?' may be the
Best question ever

The beast in all things
Was not a we
It was the heart of everything that is
My favorite work of art
Is the wooly mammoth
Drawing on the porch
All the little things
Look at all the strangers

In the newspaper
How do we recognize
What we know
Think of everyone who
Smiled at me today
Any day for that matter
Imagine all the people
And their families

Picture another land
What could freedom mean
A bike in the hedge
Odds are in your court
And the night is new
Hello, moon
Hello you
Again

PRETTY GREAT

for Sandy

Somebody calls it a wizard's tea
Somebody came and licked my knee

SEARCH ME

Yours sentimentally
When we're done doing time
Living at the zoo and
Dreaming at the movies

Future's unconditionally
At the right place
And the wrong memory

But still lives live free
But still lives still have
Lives of their own
Only eyes don't recognize

The between between
What it does and what it
Is to be

So go figure
Finger painting in the dark
Like a rumor
I don't recognize

Martians burn and...
The punch line gets tender... and... *boom*

Martians burn and...
The punch line gets tender... and... *boom*

Every moving part
Moves apart just to humor
The upper femur
Just to color

The sound of sound
A door that must be open
Or closed

The greatest caper ever
Like a furnace is just a witness
To the heat inside
The heat inside

Catastrophe is east
When you're smoking
Second hand

Conditions may apply
What's in store
Just don't breathe
Naturally

Mountains burn and...
The punch line gets tinder... and... *boom*

Mountains burn and...
The punch line gets tinder... and... *boom*

Anyone a word
When the heat arrives
Variety is a condition
Like Neapolitan skin

Spores in
Like apples and oranges
And apples again

Moon could write about
The stars all day
It's the better half of the looking glass
That has me looking back

Smudge of little hand
Into the waves again
We were just leaving

Kickflips in the halls
And I could sure use
A little air
For what I don't know

POEMS OF DEVOTION

BRAD

More often
In his own
Time than
On time
And that's
Just one
Of the things
I love about
Brad

•

NATE

A green parakeet
A sunflower
In each beak

•

GRANT

My back pages
Are yellow pages
Advertisements for
Taxidermists who
Used to drive
Taxis for a
'Living'

•

JED

A stupendous
Episode of
Cops in
Albuquerque
But you're in
Australia
Couch surfing
And suddenly
You're home
Again

•

DOUG

Can’t really
Think of
A Doug

•

DAVID

A hailstorm in
July you never
Knew you needed
Until it landed
And everyone
Stopped to
See what’s
Going on

•

MAKING A KILLING

Doesn’t really
Remind me
Of anyone
I know

•

MOON

When the moon
Winks at you
From across
The room

BELIEVE YOU ME

Odessa in your fresco
Blow a streak of
Blue in reverse

It's the pigment of the past
That draws you in
And did I mention

Hole needs an extra belt
Pick one up
While you're out

Would you pardon
The shamanic casserole
Every which way

Every switchback
Whateveryday seasons
Rearview mirror

LEST I BE A HOOKER

Thought machines of modern motion

NEVERMIND

Bring your gloves
        Holiday Inn

Tourists become
        Their final destination

Call collect
        It's personal

Crane your neck
        Warm your lungs

SELF PORTRAIT

for you

I've always
Imagined
You had a pretty
Healthy sex life
But I can't
Imagine sex
Without life
Without sex
I've always
Imagined

JUST ACT NATURAL

White noise and white suds
Sweating out the exterior
Where the weight of
The world winks back

So natural it's unbearable
The scream of prime
Numbers are like that
Home movie in burgundy

So close it's almost true
Lies are white and old
The story nods off
The deal is sealed

Numbers don't lie
Above the tree line
Sequel of rudder get
Lost on history

Outside the hotel
Riding the slopes
In the trace of arrow
Heads mention eyes

TRUE STORY

with Philip Trussell

I was a supernatural blonde
In Alexandria, 200 ADD
There's something about him…
In foresight, Promethean

There is a first time for everything
For anyone disposed by memory
Uncertainty is the ultimate spoiler
Identity will be an extinct devotion

A man pissed off the high dive
While the moon sweated and
Dogs howled and a lobster
Came swimming up the creek

The female kangaroo his three vaginas
By which better to entertain strangers
Stars fall at the same speed, a fart
Worth suspecting of history

I closed my eyes
Turned around three times and
Sometimes there's nothing to it
Never having been to Kansas

My grandfather has crossed toes
For good luck under duress…
He never knew what hit him
A luckier dog than most, maybe

There was something about her
That did something about me
Bobby Kennedy had something to say
On the black and white TV screen

I was at the peak of my career
Everything was coming up poses
Like a handplant on the edge of
A pool or a kid rolling dice

I died in September at the 7-11
Only the most recent of several times
The root of 'fact' means 'to make'
So what if science is entirely made up

We never did it together
Which I regret to this day
It looks like rain, every drop
An eye looking through me

Every tongue print is different
Not to be fingered lightly
Expect delays
While the translators get to work

Nothing didn't seem real
So something was up
Her skin was so orange
And his was so blue

TAKE THAT POEM TO CHURCH

Knock at door
But who's asking
Suede orange cabin
But who's asking
A name to go by
All arise
Knock at door

Weather shows
But never station
But who's asking
But never station
Knock at door
Repeat after me
Weather shows

On the corner
Think it over
But never station
But who's asking
A name to go by
But nothing lasts
On the corner

IN NEWPORT

My burger
Is colder
Than my beer

Chili's is the same
Everywhere

THREE POEMS

I. ORDINARY PEOPLE
Aren't average

II. PEOPLE IN LOVE
With ordinary people
Aren't average either

CASUAL MYTHOLOGY

She was from Manchester
Lived in a pink apartment
Above the yarn store

Around the corner
Her dad taught squash
Her brothers went wild

Vuarnet sunglasses and
Jams were all the rage
Then this one time

On the Slip 'n Slide
It was hot outside
Some summers last forever

We listened to The Doors
Lying on the floor
Went on and on

Cutting through
The neighbors' lawns
Then everything changed

NO PRESSURE

I.

There's this movie starring Gene Hackman I watched three times one day called *No Pressure,* where a tough, ex-football player turned private eye is hired by an aging Hollywood actress to investigate the disappearance of her promiscuous teenage daughter, Delly. Meanwhile, Moseby, the PI, discovers Ellen, his wife, is having an affair with Marty Heller. Hackman drops in on Quintin, a smart-aleck mechanic from Los Angeles, who, after getting tuned-up by Moseby, confesses that he last saw Delly on a movie set in New Mexico where she had a tryst with stuntman Marv Ellman, a former lover of the mother. Moseby flies to New Mexico to snoop around the set, and is quietly intrigued to find Quintin working on Marv's stunt-plane. Moseby has a hunch that Delly might be trying to seduce the ex-actress' ex-lovers, so he travels to the Florida Keys to meet Tom Iverson, Delly's stepfather. Down in the Keys, Mosby finds Delly living with Iverson and Paula, an attractive dolphin trainer. One night, Mosby, Delly, and Paula take a boat out for a late-night dip and discover Ellman's corpse in a crashed stunt-plane, then Delly dies in a car wreck. Suspicious of foul play, Mosby interrogates Joey, Quintin, and Ellen. The plot thickens when Quintin sleeps with the dolphins. I've been thinking about this movie a lot lately and just realized that it's actually called *Night Moves*. Sometimes it's difficult to know what one means. To be serious and know what one means.

II.

Zero gravity. And there's the store, where I refinished the floor, all tiled over. Because epistemology is for lovers, the color of color. Starfish, Starburst, starboard, a shadow's silhouette on the window. We were just waterskiing, looking for a wake, a little tape to put over the lightswitch. Watermelon, kiddie pool, side yard, there's nothing you can say that won't change the world. When I say, 'bodycams are a symptom, not a solution,' I think you feel me, into the long stretch of night driving. Somewhere in-between first waking and second sleeping, I walk slowly, like one who comes from so far away and doesn't expect to arrive. Wonder if you'd want to go for a stroll in Mt. Auburn Cemetery with me sometime? Maybe I'll even bring along some poems that are good to read under trees in a breeze.

III.
I like the way you cross your legs when you cross the street, cross-hatch patterns, gangly, like Albuquerque, the patina on Brickyard Pond, where the train tracks were, the names for things, *duende*, in a new notebook dated June six begins with a set list. You just never know. I guess that was just last week. The beer garden was closed, so I came here to swing on this swing, and write this. The difference between intuition and instinct: sometimes seeing is forgetting the name of the thing one sees.

IV.
Time has taught: remember the chalk. What time teaches: the proximity of construction sites. What time asks: remember the chalk. You never know whose heels follow whose, the pitter-patter, yes, I remember, I'd been writing some word-salady poems, and mentioned something about what I wanted to say, we just got back from the UK. You make everything look easy, and you're really a terrific tenor, so do you consider yourself a lucky man?

V.

I rang your doorbell and waited. Nobody came. So I smoked a whole pack of cigarettes on the porch and still no answer. Then I thought, 'maybe the doorbell's broken?' Then I thought, 'if I could run at the speed of sound, I could ring the bell outside, open the door, zip down the hall, and listen to see if the bell is in fact, ringing.' Then I thought, 'if I could run at the speed of sound, I wonder if I could hear anything (anything) at all?'

REPORTED SIGHTINGS

A small red helicopter
Disappears into the blue
And that's just one reason
I'm glad to know you

Hang gliders, hot air balloons
And sunfish on an open sea
Make me happy, just imagine
All the people

LOOKING AT PEOPLE

Looking at people
Looking at people

BEYOND PRONOUNS

I'm invited to an upscale lunch by one of my favorite historians. She tells me that she's just finished a new book about the history of feminism in the twentieth century.
'That's amazing, I'd really like to read it sometime.' I say.
'Well, actually, I think you're an amazing artist, and…' she says.
'Really?' Not being an artist.
'Yeah. I've always admired your work, and was wondering if you would consider illustrating my book?' She smiles and folds her napkin.
'Gosh, I'd love to. You know, I'll try anything once.'
She stares down at the table for a minute, then makes direct eye contact with me, the smile almost gone. 'I'm happy to hear that. There are just two guidelines for the images.'
I take out a pencil and say 'go ahead.'
'First, you can only use stick figures for the illustrations. No props, colors, or backgrounds. And second, after the drawings are done, you must erase all my text.'
I swirl the lime in my drinking glass.

T-BONED (NEVERMORE)

No bugs
Lots of sheep
Smells like grass
Reading *Zen and the Art of Motorcycle Maintenance*
(not so hot)
Then a cloud
And another
A light to fix
A wire to move
A place to stay put
An exit wound
It wasn't my best poem
But it wasn't mine
The water is in the air
A bicycle rolls by
A man in sunglasses
Watches a woman
Take a picture
Now the water is back
In the water
They're gone now
Back to the water
And there's a small duck
And a loud sweater
A bee bumbles by
A woman in sunglasses
Takes a picture of two girls
They're gone now
Boys smoking grass
Lay flat on their backs

In the grass
Looking up
At the clouds in the sky
And another
Is in the water
Close their eyes
The little dog frolics
A white bird circles
Another one follows
And licks its little paws
A little duck gets up
A woman blows a whistle
While she walks
Stops turns around
Something catches my eye
Especially laying down
In the sky
A man takes a picture of a woman
By the water
Back to it
Sometimes ideas of what to take a picture of
And what to skip over are hard
To skip over
Like water
It's a lot of the same
Until you get into it
And then there's a lot to process
Even when it's banal and predictable
Because that's beauty
And beauty's all about color and light
Because color is life
The boys are up from their nap
A beautiful yellow raincoat passes by
Then a butterfly
That must be the little dog
The one in the raincoat
A young monk laughs with a young woman
There's something you don't see every day

MUHAMMAD ALI

Muhammad Ali
Muhammad Ali
Muhammad Ali

STRIKING DISTANCE

for Larry Fagin

Hannah Arendt, Lester Bangs, Walter Benjamin, Wallace Berman, Carl Bernstein, Joe Brainard, Marlon Brando, Bruce Conner, Sam Cooke, Francis Ford Coppola, Arthur Danto, Angela Davis, Joan Didion, Willem de Kooning, Robert De Niro, Nick Dorsky, Bob Dylan, Peter Fonda, Paulo Freire, Hank Greenberg, Dave Hickey, Dennis Hopper, Wanda Jackson, Jasper Johns, Billie Jean King, John Lennon, John Lewis, Sergio Leone, Steve McQueen, Huey Newton, Jack Nicholson, Sam Peckinpah, Leonard Peltier, Sidney Poitier, Robert Rauschenberg, Keith Richards, Ed Ruscha, Bobby Seale, Martin Scorsese, Judee Sill, Nina Simone, Susan Sontag, Frank Stella, Hunter Thompson, Cy Twombly, Anne Waldman, Haskell Wexler, Bob Woodward, Serena Williams, Ludwig Wittgenstein, Malcolm X, Neil Young, and Howard Zinn.

SPEED QUEEN

Meg Cowen gives me a lift from the motel in Middletown to the train station in New Haven. She hands me a sack of crullers (pronounced: *kwal-las* in New England) for the ride, but I don't like sweets. In the station, Meg tells me that she invited me to Connecticut because she had a dream that we were listening to Gillian Welch on the radio driving a school bus through New Mexico. Walking down platform four, I offer the crullers to the train conductor who says, 'Thanks for the kwal-las.'

The train ride from New Haven to Boston is beachy and breezy. The phone rings and it's Ann Stephenson. She tells me Larry Fagin died earlier this morning. Look out the window at shadows and not shadows. Then I remember seeing Gillian perform at the Newport Folk Festival last summer, and Gregg Allman in a marina summer before last.

The train is passing through South County and I'm drawing pictures of Gregg and Gillian in my notebook to pass the time when I remember that Susana Gardner has a converted school bus on her family's farm that she drove to Alaska a long time ago. Or that's where it's parked in my memory, like a dream, the phone rings.

It's Nate Ethier. He tells me that Gregg Allman died earlier this morning. Look out the window at not shadows and shadows. He's up from the city somewhere in South County at a cousin's uncle's wedding or something and the train keeps moving. I'm thinking about Gregg and Larry and Nate and Ann and Gillian and Susana and Meg and the conductor.

Catch a ride from Back Bay to North Station. A driftwood sculptor from Maine picks me up. Cash only but no problem. It's his day off. Killing time by the Charles River I try to remember the names of all the people I met last summer in Somerville. Looking at a big green sign that says Somerville. Then I remember that memory lane can be a dead end street and buy a one-way ticket to Gloucester. And a cup of coffee.

And think how much I'd like to walk around Cambridge with you. Now or forty years ago. Take the commuter rail to the second to last stop. The graveyards near the train tracks are old but unsanctioned as if age alone made them refined and weedy.

I think about visiting Bob Creeley's grave last summer, and that graveyard is also old and refined but devoid of weeds and totally sanctioned. Then Amanda Cook gives me a lift from the train station to Vincent Ferrini's old frame shop where I'll be staying for the week.

Amanda gives me the key and I ask if I need sign anything or anything. 'No,' she says, 'Just don't be an asshole.' I love New England. We make plans to have lunch with Gerrit Lansing and she writes down Henry Ferrini's phone number.

Now it's cold and pissing rain and I'm out of clothes so I go out looking for a laundromat. I stop by the harbor and think about Bob and Charles Olson looking at the same water together a very long time ago. Apparently Bobbie Louise Hawkins has some super-eight footage from their first visit to Olson's. I'd like to see that with you sometime.

I stumble on a laundromat just a quarter mile down the street and load the wash and load the quarters and wash a load. I'm already soaked so I take a walk to kill time and wander into an antique store on a pier. The shop has a bunch of sturdy old wool jackets and flannels and I scoop them up along with a book about psychedelic concert posters.

The guy at the register, a handsome guy at the register, tells me that the book is not for sale. Turns out this is Bob Driscoll and he has some poster work for the Boston Tea Party featured in that very book. He shows me some examples, including a poster he made for the Allman Brothers. I ask him if he's heard the news. We talk art and music for a very long time and watch the rain.

I try to square up with Bob but it's cash only which is a problem because I left my cash at Vincent's. 'No problem,' he says, 'Take the clothes and pay me back when you have a chance.' I layer on all the clothes and walk back to the Laundromat.

I'm feeling warmer and dryer and put the clothes in the dryer and walk to a restaurant next door. Inside, there's a poem on the wall by Bob (that's Bob Creeley, not Driscoll) that goes like this:

> Love comes quietly
> finally, drops
> about me, on me,
> in the old ways
>
> What did I know
> thinking myself
> able to go
> alone all the way

Funny to see a friend's poem, or any poem, in a restaurant. I order a hot stew and chat up the bartender, who happens to have just moved from Austin to Gloucester. Her husband and I like the same bakery, Easy Tiger. Later that night Susana calls to see if I'd like to get together the next day. As we're talking I walk by a ship named Susannah. Back at Vincent's I fix the stereo, put on *Eat a Peach*, lay down on the floor, close my eyes, wondering what to make of it all.

WHAT DO MOVIE STARS DO ALL DAY

Wear sunglasses at night
Drive convertibles with scarves wrapped around their heads
Put cucumber slices over their eyes
Drink martinis with three olives
Walk down red carpets in evening gowns
Take bubble baths
Order room service on silver trays
Begin and end sentences with 'darling'
Stay in the best hotels
Say, 'I'm feeling faint'
Faint
Catch other movie stars who faint
Excuse themselves for 'urgent calls'
Flee the paparazzi
Drink red punch with orange slices
See pictures of themselves in the morning paper
Bite their fists
Say, 'follow that car' and 'step on it'
Hire private eyes
Confide in their agents

TEXAS

Like death
Warmed over

A NEW KIND OF COUNTRY

Can't talk knife out of
Feel like riding
Instead a sweet dreams
Inways indigo concede
For the cicadas
Feel like riding
For the cicadas

Most of the times
I just don't get it
Earth rooms around a
Camera call a satellite
Mingle like a natural
I just don't get it
Mingle like a natural

About the chairs
Fold back in time
With sirens always on
Ease by degree
A head of curve
Fold back in time
A head of curve

Body's shape time
T-bird on tube
Pass the mind
To your left brain
Scratch marks you back
T-bird on tube
Scratch marks you back

Motion as a verb
Sound not a word
Like wild jasmine
A long way here
Which way is America
Sound not a word
Which way is America

DEBUT

My poetics is the hardest part. There's nothing impersonal about these poems. But that's not the hardest part. Never knew if all this noodling would amount to much, that is, until I got my big break. After I got my chops down I saw fit for appearances, but things aren't always what they seem. Poems have taught me you can just look over there at that and tell someone you trust. Catch on eventually, while all the time. Then you hit the ceiling while the sky is falling. Other times a wink is just a blink marked by intention.

I read the poems. It's morning. I used the last of the soap and went outside. I took a ride. The drugs in my mind put me at ease while the drugs in my past differentiate. My poems are sincere: it was the hardest year of my life, for me personally, to be a person. Hours pass and I collect my belongings. To a certain extent, life's all about planning for the future while being totally in the present. In the new age we'll still be skin and bones, so I hit the road. It was nice seeing you at the museum, but what I wanted more than anything was take a swim from one end of the spring to the other. And a glass of water. You can picture it. Now turn the picture. I swam the other way. And back again.

Later I'm supposed to meet somebody somewhere. A mutual friend believe it or not. But they're not there. Danger says hello. Lately I've been having a hard time remembering people I meet in social contexts. I have a lot of anxiety in social settings, but when I get nervous I get loquacious. That's intensely personal and honest, yet professional to a degree and politically self-conscious at best, but not for lack of trying to get to the crux of what aware means and seldom.

Fact of the matter is people describe me as charming, yet colloquial and pleasant. Easy on the eyes and ears and that soothes the mind and calms the heart. Good stuff, I think to myself, and but not without an innate sense of privacy and belonging, which fits the personality. Which fits the person and the day-to-day upkeep of running around and folding things like towels and chairs, hands and arms, with an earnest sense of purpose and well-being. I know this about myself, but getting to know myself is part of the routine, like reading, meditation, and swimming. That's just a for instance.

Anyway, I shot some pool with your friend Tony. What a nice guy, I think to myself. Then that missing someone I mentioned earlier appears in the doorway. It was almost dusk. We made plans to take a walk but that never happened and that's worth remembering because of what I said earlier about being totally present and planning for the future. What a nice day, I think to myself later lying on the floor covered in clay. I close my eyes and read the poems, which brings me back to the hardest part.

So what do I do with my poetics? I'm working on my relic and I occasionally need poetics for it, but it's such a small amount. My consciousness as a storyteller and writer comes from the land because I am the land. I have described my poetics as a poetics of collision and as lyric conceptualism, but that won't be a thing you consider for a while. My objective in these lines is to notice the points without recognizing me in the least. I've lolled with lists that verse demands, nevertheless my ambitious plan is to improve my skills and provide you with a few bearable pieces. The instrument I am developing is a grand piano with electronic augmentations. I rolled up my sleeves after taking a seat and adapted the strings to cater to my poetics. To put it mildly, it's just twelve-tone music, but easier on the ears. Someone once said, poetry is the only means I have of saying anything positive about the world, and I think to myself, That's a sad, sad state of affairs. On a related note, I once read a slogan for an MFA program in Wyoming that claimed to be, The last refuge for poetry, and I thought, What an awful place that must be.

My best work is occupying several dimensions simultaneously. I was talking briefly on a small panel about my poetics recently, so I had to think again about what poetics meant. It's one of those plural words that's provisional at best, a poetics of drought, an attention to what is proximal, nearby, accessible. I cannot separate my body, my identity, from my poetics, since my admiration is grounded, in part, upon a newfound interest in lyrical experimentalism. More on that later.

First, I must disclose a seismic shift in my poetics. While my poetry and prose is written without fear, my poetics is terrified, a stray fringe of woven cloth, unincorporated bits, ragged edges comprised of the phone calls I can't return, the emails that stutter, all the events that stand out without a past or a future. What I'm really talking about is interruption, the disquieting rungs of life slipping by over coffee with someone I trust.

My poetics is simple, and that's the hardest part. For example, sign and signifier are very important to me because I think we should employ the full capacity (or a limited capacity, fully) of both language and the world, like a walk with a smart dog does. The friend I mentioned earlier and I had the same political positions but our poetics were totally different. Ron Silliman critiqued my declarative categorization, calling my poetics simply transgressive, i.e., not evil in an ethical sense since these practices are representative of my poetics, a quote-unquote matter of making art out of words, because experimentation, the unequivocal personal as the political transparency of erasure, has meaning. That's all I'm really getting at: does language really need a body? One of the niceties of art is not having to say yes or no but why? I mean, the whole universe is humming, it's vibrating, and it's that hum that I want to hear. My poetics are informed by my daily psychic negotiations with culture. My new book opens with this poem:

I wanted my foot in all of them
Specifically because I like everybody
At every level there's a desire

An ancient desire of transcendence
A steppingstone in the evolution
Striving to claim some authenticity

Giving my authority to a universal
Variable where nothing stands for
Nothing other than what it is

Like in How I Got to Memphis
Patterns and colors without symmetry
If you love somebody enough

If I had to sum up my poetics in one word, it would be interiority. But we all know one word doesn't mean anything. That's why my friend from the museum and I wrote a hundred one-word poems last week. I write to prove a point to myself, but also to be quietly entertained. Poetry saves time and money. We are, almost as a reflex, destructive to the labyrinthine structure of mediation, convincing me that my poetics cannot be separated from my inability to take academics as seriously as they take themselves. But people do have ideas, like they say. Yes, people do have ideas.

Deciding which books to give to the Goodwill and which books to buy and which books to read will also tell you a thing or two about what someone is made of. For example, I resolved to get rid of most of my poetry books a few years back, but I'm not naming names. Not now. When it comes down to it, my poetics seems straight forward enough. Nothing new really. I do talk a lot about such things. That's the nerves talking. There's so much great poetry in the world. More than I could read in a lifetime, which makes me wonder why anyone wants to make more of it? Maybe that's one to avoid mulling over when you're feeling blue? Maybe not. But that's beside the point.

I have been described as a late modernist, and although I'm not sure I want to be referred to as late, it's true that my poetics began with a reading of Ezra Pound, but I don't want my poems to have a uniform quality. I talk about process a lot because I'm always processing and sometimes I wish I could just turn it off and go to a canyon. I should add that I view my poetics as operating across languages. I came to believe in a poetics of mutation and then I lost my poetics somewhere along the way. In the pool or canyon or deep in meditation. Because I have a tendency toward getting to know someone with as little conversation as possible, which can come off as affection, but it's just the economy. I want a poem that's as casual as it is deep and light without catering to the usual suspects.

I'm too old to be experimental, to face the internal realities of those seduced with the jargon of condescension because it's evaporating even if you can't see it. I once wrote a poem in real time about watching a mighty river become a dreary canyon just to see if it was possible, but just as I was about to wrap it up the batteries died and I had to seek out new forms of energy, so I put five thousand years of ecological poetics into dialogue with a decade of new media poetics to see what would happen. The jury's still out on that one.

It is that, to some misleading degree, but not, entirely to my mind, in good enough keeping with the positioning of a writing desk in a public social space. When I lived in Colorado I built a desk and chair heavy enough to place in a mighty river without washing away downstream. It kept my legs cool but the poems of that period weren't so hot. It's personal, and possible to be grandiose and at times extravagant, enchanted by the irrelevant place poetry occupies in the world, but you could say that about anything.

So in conclusion, it's also worth mentioning what I've been working on in the last three weeks is a sudden and unexpected digression from the usual. Because it's current. There was nothing that needed pressing. Some people would doubtless think to call my poetics postmodern. It is that, to some misleading degree, but not, to my mind, in good enough keeping with the tradition of history. One question I'll leave you with today would thus be how to re-inscribe that older, now lost mode, the middle voice into the poem. Eventually my relationships with people and the land affected my poetics because I wanted to be astonished and atonal, so I became more experimental. It didn't last long, because I'd like to write something contingent and inductive based on a stubborn desire to put one foot in front of another to create as powerful an aesthetic experience as I can summon. Like Tom Hall said, If you love somebody enough, you'll follow wherever they go. And that's how I got to Memphis.

HERE'S THE THING

Feelings have feelings
Bodies have bodies
Ideas have ideas
Spirits have spirits
Thoughts have thoughts
Emotions have emotions

Feelings have bodies
Feelings have ideas
Feelings have spirits
Feelings have thoughts
Feelings have emotions
Feelings have feelings

Bodies have ideas
Bodies have spirits
Bodies have thoughts
Bodies have emotions
Bodies have feelings
Bodies have bodies

Ideas have spirits
Ideas have thoughts
Ideas have emotions
Ideas have feelings
Ideas have bodies
Ideas have ideas

Spirits have thoughts
Spirits have emotions

Spirits have feelings
Spirits have bodies
Spirits have ideas
Spirits have spirits

Thoughts have emotions
Thoughts have feelings
Thoughts have bodies
Thoughts have ideas
Thoughts have spirits
Thoughts have thoughts

Emotions have feelings
Emotions have bodies
Emotions have ideas
Emotions have spirits
Emotions have thoughts
Emotions have emotions

Emotions have emotions
Thoughts have thoughts
Spirits have spirits
Ideas have ideas
Bodies have bodies
Feelings have feelings

WILD DELIGHT

On any given Monday
Hookshot in driveway
You know, just ask Randy
On any given Monday

You know, just ask Randy
Play cool, but not too
On any given Monday
Hookshot in driveway

•

Odds are your angle
Money under table
Put boots up on thigh
Odds are your angle

Put boots up on thigh
The sisters go backwards
Odds are your angle
Money under table

•

Shades down afternoon
Inspired by actual story
Full of hearts and stars
Shades down afternoon

Full of hearts and stars
Longer layover the better
Shades down afternoon
Inspired by actual story

•

Hands up money down
Snuggle into bed forget
Walk around dock
Hands up money down

Walk around dock
Barking at thunder
Hands up money down
Snuggle into bed forget

•

Something something it's you
Gather wood for fire
Something gotta give it's rain
Something something it's you

Something gotta give it's rain
Sucking up to the atmosphere
Something something it's you
Gather wood for fire

•

Better for year-round feeding
Prefer water from well
Know it? I destroyed it
Better for year-round feeding

Know it? I destroyed it
Double-cross universe
Better for year-round feeding
Prefer water from well

•

Headlong into future
Forget I stopped to remember
Associate speedwagon
Headlong into future

Associate speedwagon
Winner by a nuzzle
Headlong into future
Forget I stopped to remember

•

Strip down saddle up
What's in it for dreams
Angst mortal sins
Strip down saddle up

Angst mortal sins
Recite in slow-mo
Strip down saddle up
What's in it for dreams

HOW COLOR WORKS

for Nate Ethier

An afternoon balloon floats
Through an open door
Helium the color of anon
You can picture it

The form is imposed
And when you lift it
It goes up, up, up
Through the social world

And out into the street
Where gravity is a noun
And always on
Past the brick and vine

The temperature is
Medium cool
But familiar
The color of Tempranillo

A grotto spilling sideways
As if color were an alias
By any other name
Discontinuous movement

Blows the door closed
To keep the light in
To fill a room with light
And render a wilderness

Perpendicular yet colloquial
The color of wilderness
You remember best
Goes on in green

Which like rain
Can only astonish clearly
As if ascension
And rain again

OUTSIDE THE WORD BALLOON

for Bill Berkson

Candid paths crossing
This way and that
An iron-on winter rain

Jackknifes through trees
Effortless smile

Such capable hands
Sublime scribble
Bending the wind

Turrets of excess
Overlook eucalyptus

Baroque
To the nines
It's happened to me

As far as eyes twinkle
Where the chairs

Reconfigure the stars
As the curtain falls
Like a corkscrew

All of you
Mountain view

NONE OF US

with Ted Greenwald

Beam me a zinger
Beautiful beauty parlor
Best backup singers

•

Bud leaf shadows
Red brick w/ pompom
Window blotters

•

Sunset strip
Clams rubbernose
Loosey goosey placebo

•

Any simple animals walk by
They're people
The very people

•

Halcyon days scratch surface
So surmised is a sentence
Angels' braincells

•

Beyond Sound Bite Valley
Tundra-ing hoofs
Rush hour whistling snowflakes

•

Wranglers vortex
Limestone landslide parade dog
Better run for it

•

No
Not either

Nothing

•

Where wildflowers stand taller
Than me if I can't feel you
I have nothing to say to you

•

No money
No money
No money

•

There's nothing more beautiful
Than two beautiful people
Making something beautiful together

•

Four seasons day
Folder lies empty
Talking paints

•

Beachball tumbleweed
Across a city sleep
Citizens denizens

•

Kinda looks
Been and gone swatches
Watch mop

•

Tingle in the right arm
Chalkdust mouth
Think I'll pack it in and buy a pickup

•

Across USA
Cross out weather
So waitressing about this

•

Wide awake and breathing hard
Green that is green that is green
Like there's no tomorrow resemble

•

Singer
A diff tune
Thou T so

•

Comes a time
Birds of paradise
Comes a time

•

Calling all clouds
Country of origin
End user certificate

•

Pack it away no if ands or
But about in the
Tall grass tomorrow

•

5th in out
Anything on road
Let's go faces

•

Everyday losers
Camel careening toward natch
Batten down the hatch

•

Weather inventory
Today, do clouds
Today's done clouds

•

Everything was groovy
On the magic sleighride
Then something happened

•

Happens yester
The at first
Hot later later

•

One step
And another
And another

•

Ah…
It…
Could work

•

Time being
Hover light
Water over water

•

Nose on mind
Knife handwriting
Little kick

•

My favorite picture of you
Watching the birds
A potato in the sky

•

Drive off in my hair
At foot of seal legs
Feel like family

•

Light change
The feeling that happens
In so many words

•

Little bird
Where is
Your little song

•

Camera clicks
Light both ends
Clouds cattle land

•

Sit around talking
Snowflake blossoms
Dicey

•

Oui the people
It's personal
Another human

•

Bird jumping
And flapping
Be my beloved

•

Misery scatters
About beauty
Take fire

•

Air across face
As eye they close
In an grammar

•

Heavy air
More barn
Stroke of genius

•

How this ends
The best restrooms
None of us

Kyle Schlesinger is a poet, printer, and professor. His publications include *A New Kind of Country* (Chax Press, 2020), *Color & Light* (Dusie, 2020), *None of Us,* a collaboration with Ted Greenwald (Kin Press, 2020), *Vast Acid West,* a collaboration with Crane Giamo (Cuneiform Press/ Pocalypstic Editions, 2020), and *A Poetics of the Press* (Ugly Duckling Presse, 2020). He resides in Austin, where he serves as the proprietor of Cuneiform Press.

Twenty-six copies of the first print edition of
A New Kind of Country are lettered and signed by the author.

Founded in 1984 in Tucson, Arizona, Chax Press has published more than 240 books in a variety of formats, including handprinted letterpress books and chapbooks, hybrid chapbooks, book arts editions, and trade paperback editions such as the book you are holding. From August 2014 until July 2018 Chax Press resided in the University of Houston-Victoria Center for the Arts. Individual donors have supported *A New Kind of Country*. Chax is a nonprofit 501(c)(3) organization which depends on suppport from various government & private funders, and, primarly, from individual donors and readers. In July 2018 Chax Press returned to Tucson, Arizona.

Our current address is 1517 North Wilmot Road no. 264, Tucson, Arizona 85712-4410. You can email us at *chaxpress@chax.org.*

You may find CHAX at *https://chax.org*

You may also find many readings by our authors, as well as our podcasts and other endeavors online at *https://www.youtube.com/channel/UCxUXE-_zgL8acZC6-K2obzg/*